David Crosweller

THE STORY OF

Buddhism

CONNECTIONS
BOOK PUBLISHING

A CONNECTIONS EDITION

This edition published in Great Britain in 2000 by
Connections Book Publishing Limited
St Chad's House
148 King's Cross Road
London WC1X 9DH

British Library Cataloguing-in-Publication data is
available on request.

ISBN 1-85906-045-5

1 3 5 7 9 10 8 6 4 2

Phototypeset in Bible Script and Berkeley
Oldstyle using QuarkXPress on Apple Macintosh
Origination by Bright Arts PTE, Singapore
Printed and bound by C & C Offset
Printing Co. Ltd, Hong Kong

Contents

⊙ LEFT *Perhaps for this Buddhist
monk in Polonnaruwa, Sri Lanka,
daily worship at the feet of the
Buddha is a reflection of his practice.*

What is Buddhism?

Buddhism is a tradition that offers all individuals, regardless of religious persuasion, a way of exploring the true role and purpose of our lives as human beings. The tradition takes its name from the word 'Buddha', which means 'the awakened one'. Put simply, the goal of Buddhists is to awaken to the true nature of reality. This is not just an intellectual process; rather, it is one which engages the whole person and typically involves the awakening of the heart just as much as the mind.

There is a particular story that is familiar in Buddhist teachings. In this story, four men (sometimes it is said they are blind) are asked to feel a strange animal in the darkness and identify it. The first man feels its head, the second its ear, the third its tusk and the fourth its tail, and each exclaims that they know what it is, pronouncing 'it' to be a pot, a winnowing fan, a plough and a broom respectively. The Buddha used this story to illustrate the life we all endure, and the views held by some of his more animated followers. He said:

'Those people, blind, unseeing, without knowing the truth, each maintain that it is like this and like that.'

Although many volumes of literature have accumulated over the centuries based on the teachings of the Buddha, Buddhism is essentially a non-dogmatic religion. The Buddha himself wrote down not a word, and the first validated texts were recorded some four hundred years after his death.

⊙ MAIN PICTURE *In the Himalayas of Nepal, standing at 4,400 metres, rising through the clouds the monastery steeple stands watching, waiting.*

Although a number of different interpretations of his teachings have evolved over the centuries, there are certain basic principles to which all Buddhist schools subscribe (more about these later). However, none of them prescribe a specific set of beliefs; rather, they stress the fundamental importance of direct religious experience.

Many Buddhist practices offer ways of exploring and responding to the kind of questions that have preoccupied people for centuries: 'Who am I?', 'Why am I here?' and 'What is life for, and what does it mean?'. The basis of Buddhist teaching is not about what to believe; it is about what we can do to deepen our understanding of ourselves, and in so doing learn how to penetrate the mystery at the heart of life.

I recommend that you read through the rest of this booklet before you begin to use the cards. This will give you insight into the story and practice of Buddhism, and help you to better understand how to meditate on the reflection cards and mandala in this pack.

The Buddha's Life

The man who was to become known as 'the Buddha' was born around 563 BCE in the foothills of the Himalayas, on the northern edge of the plain of the river Ganges. One of the earliest accounts of his life was recorded by a Sanskrit poet, Ashvaghosha, during either the first or second century CE, and is known as the 'Buddhacarita', or 'Acts of the Buddha'. Many biographies followed, but no version of the Buddha's life and work was recorded anywhere close to the time in which he lived; some of the claims about his story, therefore, may well be embellishments. The most popular version of events now follows.

Childhood Years

The Buddha was born as Siddhartha Gautama to a prominent family of the Shakya clan, who occupied the foothills of the Himalayas. Siddhartha's family lived in the capital city, Kapilavastu. Some accounts of Siddhartha's early life state that his father, Suddhodhana, was king of the Shakyas, but he may simply have been an important citizen.

Before Siddhartha was conceived, his mother, Mahamaya, dreamed that she was visited by a marvellous white elephant. When she gave birth, she experienced no pain at all, and it is said that streams of water poured from the heavens to wash her and her baby. Then the newly born infant rose up of his own accord and strode northwards with seven sturdy strides, announcing, 'I am the chief of the world, I am the best in the world, I am the first in the world. This is my last birth. There is now no existence again.' Just one week after the birth, Mahamaya died, and Siddhartha was entrusted to her sister, Mahapajapati.

Shortly after this, an elderly sage called Asita visited Suddhodhana's palace. When he saw the infant Siddhartha, he immediately recognized that he was looking on a child destined to be a great spiritual leader. Asita wept, telling Suddhodhana that his tears were not out of sorrow for the child, but pity for himself, for he knew he would not live long enough to experience the child's teachings.

Suddhodhana was delighted that his child was destined for leadership of a high

⊙ LEFT *The terraced foothills of the Himalayas where Siddhartha Gautama, the Buddha, was born.*
⊙ ABOVE *This relief carving is one of the 1,460 carved panels found on the terraces of Borobudur in Java, the largest Buddhist monument in the world. The carvings depict scenes from the life of Buddha; this one is thought to depict the Buddha's mother, Mahamaya, before she gave birth.*

⊙ ABOVE *This 18th-century print is believed to depict the Buddha's journey from birth to enlightenment.*

So Siddhartha enjoyed a luxurious upbringing in Kapilavastu, hermetically protected from the outside world. As a youth, he was everything his father hoped for: handsome, intelligent and a master of many sports. When he grew to manhood, he married a beautiful young woman, Yasodhara, who bore him a son, Rahula.

But by the time he was approaching his thirtieth year, Siddhartha began to question what happened beyond the city walls. He struck an agreement with his groom, Channa, and together they went on four secret excursions. On the first, they encountered an old man; on the second, a sick one; and on the third, a corpse being prepared for cremation. Siddhartha's view of the world was suddenly and irrevocably shattered. For the first time in his life, he began to grasp the true facts of the human condition: everyone – rich, powerful, poor or weak – is susceptible to illness, old age and death. And then …? He knew that he

order, but he wanted a son who would find greatness as a warrior or political leader, not as a saint. To ensure the boy's mind would not turn towards religion, he resolved to educate him in such a way that he would never encounter the painful or ugly side of life. He reasoned that if Siddhartha had all he could wish for, he would not be prompted to look beyond the pleasures surrounding him.

⊙ MAIN PICTURE *A monk on a journey to the Dhanhar monastery in Spiti, India. Walking has long been the accepted way for monks to move from place to place. A good time to contemplate.*

could not stay in Kapilavastu and ignore what he had seen. He had to find out more.

Siddhartha's Search

On the fourth expedition with Channa, Siddhartha saw a sadhu, a wandering sage, dressed in rags. When Channa told him that this sadhu was one of many holy men who seek to unravel the mysteries of life by rejecting the comforts of the material world, Siddhartha decided that this was the path he too must follow. He arranged with Channa to escape from Kapilavastu by dead of night. The two men rode to the border of the Shakya kingdom, and Siddhartha crossed the river into the neighbouring kingdom of Magadha, where he soon encountered another sadhu. Siddhartha cut off his long black hair and gave his clothes to the sadhu in return for the sadhu's thin, saffron robe. Then he set out to find a teacher.

Siddhartha found his way to two of the most distinguished spiritual leaders of the day, Alara Kalama and Uddha Ramaputtra. But although the two men were able to teach him many helpful meditation practices, he did not feel that either had helped him to resolve the heart of his problem. So he decided to focus on a life of strict asceticism, in the hope that if he subjected his body to the most extreme forms of suffering, he would be able to overcome suffering itself. He lived with five companions who were also intent on pursuing the ascetic path; he slept on beds of thorns and starved himself until he could touch his backbone through the skin of his belly. But still he did not solve his problem. He also realized that if he continued such extreme practices, he risked dying before finding a solution. But what were his options? He had

⊙ MAIN PICTURE *This sacred bodhi tree, believed to be over two thousand years old, is found in the ancient site of Anuradapura, Sri Lanka.*

⊙ BELOW *This 18th-century tangka shows Mara, the god of death and desire. The Buddha overcame Mara's two attributes on his way to enlightenment.*

rejected a life of material luxury and had not made the progress he hoped for with a life of renunciation and poverty.

As he struggled with his dilemma, Siddhartha overheard the instructions of a fisherman who was teaching the lute to a young boy. 'If you wind the strings too tight, they will snap,' the fisherman explained, 'whereas if you leave them too loose, the lute will not play. But when the strings are just right – not too loose and not too tight – you can start to make music.'

Listening to these instructions, Siddhartha realized that there was another path available to him: the Middle Way. But when he told his five companions that he intended to renounce fasting and try another method, he was scorned by them. So he set out on the next stage of his search alone. At a place called Bodh Gaya, in the modern Indian state of Bihar, he made himself a cushion of grass beneath the branches of a bodhi tree. He resolved to sit in meditation here until he found an answer to the problem of suffering.

Siddhartha's actions and resolve were watched with mounting alarm by Mara, lord of the demons and master of the illusory world. Mara's role in the scheme of things is to tempt humans to believe that there is nothing beyond the repeating cycle of birth, death and rebirth. When he saw how close Siddhartha had come to breaking through the illusory veils that surrounded him,

Mara staged an all-out assault. He sent armies of hideous demons, but Siddhartha was unmoved. He sent each of his seductive daughters, but Siddhartha was again unmoved. Finally, Mara had to admit defeat. Siddhartha had entered the state of *samadhi*, or enlightenment, and in this state he made actions are reborn in misery, while those who acquire good karma through generous actions are reborn to happiness. Finally, he gained mastery of all kinds of addiction: sensual desire, mortal life and ignorance.

In the terms of modern science, we could say that Siddhartha had experienced

⊙ FAR LEFT *A young monk and an old lama journey through the Himalayas on their way to Zanshar in Kashmir, India.*

⊙ LEFT *Two Buddhist nuns contemplate the breathtaking view in Chiwong Gompa, Nepal.*

three crucial discoveries. First, he remembered his former lives; second, he understood the workings of karma and saw how those who acquire bad karma through evil the manifest world as an outpouring of energy from a mysterious, unlimited source. Once his mind was perfectly quiet and still, he could feel the presence of this energy

within the depths of his own being and in all animate life forms around him. This, he understood, was his true nature. When Siddhartha came out of his final confrontation with Mara, he was no longer Siddhartha. He had become the Buddha, the Awakened One. Leaning forward, he touched the earth to bear witness to his achievement.

The Buddha's Ministry

The Buddha is said to have remained in meditation under the bodhi tree for several weeks. Blissful though he was, he felt sure it would be impossible to convey his discovery to others. Then he was visited by the Hindu god Brahma Sahampati, who told him that there were some people with 'just a little dust in their eyes'. The Buddha's sense of compassion was stirred and he agreed to help them see clearly.

The first people the Buddha sought out were the five ascetics who had

⊙ LEFT *The Hindu god Vishnu, the preserver – the deity who has transformed himself into Rama, Krishna and, according to Hindus, the Buddha.*

spurned him when he gave up his fight against hunger. As soon as he approached them, they could see at once that he had undergone a complete spiritual transformation. When he started to teach them about the Middle Way and the truths he had discovered, one of them, Kondanna, understood him at once. Kondanna became the first Buddhist monk, or bhikkhu. Soon afterwards the remaining four ascetics were also ordained, and the first Buddhist community, or Sangha, was formed.

The Buddha was about thirty-five years old when he became enlightened. He continued to teach until his death at about eighty. During those years, he walked tirelessly across northern India, teaching to whoever was willing to listen and drawing no distinction between race, caste, sex or vocation. He was apparently an inspiring figure, for many people who heard him speak were immediately ready to give up their former lives and devote themselves to following him. Before long, the number of mass conversions prompted the Buddha to set up a formal ordination procedure. This involved making three simple vows: These three concepts of Buddha, Dharma (teaching) and Sangha (order or community) are collectively referred to as 'the three jewels'.

I take my refuge in the Buddha
I take my refuge in the Dharma
I take my refuge in the Sangha

Later, the Buddha introduced a more detailed monastic code. Like him, his monks led a homeless life, wandering from place to place. As the message of Buddhism spread, more donations were offered to the monks, and many lay communities were established. The principle of exchange between lay people and monks has been a hallmark of Buddhism ever since: monks may receive food, shelter, clothing, medicine and other necessities, offering the teachings in return.

Inevitably, the Buddha found his way back to Kapilavastu. When he taught there,

⊙ MAIN PICTURE *Looming large above the worshippers, this is the head section of Daibutsu (Great Buddha), which is found in Kamakura, Japan.*

large numbers of people converted, among them his younger brother Nanda, and son Rahula. His cousin, Ananda, also converted to Buddhism and would be his faithful attendant during the latter part of his life.

During the fifth year of the Buddha's ministry, Suddhodhana died. The Buddha's aunt, Mahapajapati, asked him to ordain her. When he refused, she cut off her hair, put on the saffron robes of the renunciate, and followed him with a group of female companions. At last, the Buddha agreed to ordain her, but he laid down eight stringent requirements, one of which was that a nun – bhikkhuni – would always be junior even to a recently ordained monk, and must defer to him. However, he is also recorded as having said to Ananda that both women and men have the same spiritual potential.

The rapid growth and high morale of the Buddhist Sangha attracted the envy of other religious sects in India. However, the Buddha's ministry was characterized by tolerance and liberality and by exceptional skills as a peacemaker, both within the Buddhist community and with other religious sects. In fact, modern Hindus do not regard the Buddha as an outsider, but as a manifestation of the great god Vishnu, the preserver, who descends to the world in particularly difficult times to set things right.

The Final Year

The last year of the Buddha's life is recorded in some detail and his death has become a myth in its own right. While the Buddha was visiting a town called Pava, he was given a meal by Cunda the smith that triggered his fatal illness. Despite the ravaging effects of the poison that was in the meal, he and his companions went on their way to the village of Kusinari, but he was so racked with pain by the time they reached the village outskirts that he had to stop and rest. As he left this life, it is said that the sala trees rained blossom, even though it was out of

season, and that the gods of all of the world systems gathered around him in such a dense crowd that a hair could not be slipped between them. In every sphere of existence, there was grieving, among animals and gods as well as among humans. Even as he died, the Buddha continued to teach, and his last words were addressed to a local ascetic named Subhada: *'All created things are impermanent. Strive on mindfully.'*

⊙ ABOVE *Even on his death bed, the Buddha continued teaching. Once his being had left his body, the body was cremated, and this 18th-century image portrays the final days leading up to this event.*

The Buddha's Teachings

The Four Noble Truths

The root of the Buddha's teaching is the doctrine of the four noble truths:

- *Suffering exists*
- *Suffering has an identifiable cause*
- *The cause of suffering can be terminated*
- *There are specific ways in which the cause can be terminated*

Freedom from suffering brings about the state of nirvana. There are two kinds of nirvana. The first has a residual basis – an example of this is the state of nirvana that the Buddha attained underneath the bodhi tree. The second has no residual basis – for example, the state the Buddha entered when he finally passed away.

As nirvana lies beyond our normal sphere of experience and is a state of *being* rather than a state of mind, it is impossible to describe in words. But one record of the Buddha's teaching expresses it as a state in which, 'There is neither earth, nor air, nor fire, nor water; there is no consciousness, nor space, nor void, nor perception, nor non-perception. There is neither a coming nor a going, neither a standing still nor a falling away, without being fixed, nor without moving, nor without basis. It is the end of suffering.'

The practical steps we may take in order to prepare ourselves for the state in which nirvana can arise are explained in the doctrine of the Noble Eightfold Path.

⊙ ABOVE *The Buddha achieved perfect enlightenment through meditation, and this Tibetan statue of him seated on a lotus is the image of calm and serenity.*

The Noble Eightfold Path

The Eightfold Path is subdivided into three further elements (*see below*), all of which need to be combined when following the Noble Path. These elements are regarded as essential aspects of the way to reach enlightenment.

◇

THE EIGHTFOLD PATH

- Right Understanding
- Right Thought
- Right Speech
- Right Action
- Right Livelihood
- Right Effort
- Right Mindfulness
- Right Concentration

- WISDOM
- MORALITY
- MEDITATION

◇

⊙ ABOVE *The sacred mantras so fundamental to Buddhist thought can be found carved into rock, such as this one on the Kora Path in Lhasa, Tibet.*

WISDOM

Wisdom is inherent in Right Understanding: in order to practise the teachings we need to be acquainted with the Four Noble Truths and to have started to penetrate their meaning by testing them against experience. Wisdom is also inherent in Right Thought – the motive of the practitioner must not be personal salvation, but a selfless willingness to work in the interests of the well-being of others. Further, devotion to the Middle Way requires that we change our attitude from a self-centred orientation to one that is more altruistic, tolerant and benign. Right Thought is also the foundation of Right Action: Buddhist practice is not about disengaging from the world, but rather about helping to create a better one.

MORALITY

Buddhism does not prescribe a rigid moral code but it does offer guidelines. Morality is inherent in Right Speech, which is about

⊙ MAIN PICTURE *The hand of Padmasambhava, the Tibetan saint credited with ensuring that Buddhist teachings took root in Tibet. In his hand he holds a vajra – a symbolic wrathful object for dispelling negativity.*

not lying, gossiping or backbiting, and in general about not using speech in wasteful or harmful ways. It is also about being open and truthful. Morality is also inherent in Right Action, which concerns decent behaviour. The Five Precepts of Right Action are:

To live a life free from harming any living beings

To live a life free from stealing or taking what is not ours

To live a life free from abusing the senses

To live a life free from telling any kind of untruth

To live a life free from self-intoxication with alcohol or drugs

Finally, morality is inherent in Right Livelihood. This means bringing integrity to our work and being clear about our motives in working; the Buddhist practitioner does not work to get rich quick; rather, the emphasis is on working in a way that does not harm others or pollute the world. This leads directly to Right Effort. Although Buddhism advocates tolerance, it also requires that we make the effort to stay

⊙ RIGHT *Buddhist monks in the temple of Bayon in Angkor, Cambodia. Completed at the end of the 12th century, this awe-inspiring temple boasts two hundred stone faces which gaze out in all directions.*

mindful and alert and so be fully aware of the effect of our actions. The term 'engaged Buddhism' describes Buddhist morality in action – it is a way of extending compassion outside one's own personal sphere into a wider framework such as social or community work, or environmental campaigning.

MEDITATION

Meditation is encompassed by Right Mindfulness and Right Concentration. By meditating, the Buddhist practitioner refines his or her appreciation and understanding of the Buddha's teachings. Meditation is not to be pursued for selfish motives such as mind power or peak experiences; it is to be regarded as a serious practice and is best followed under the guidance of a committed and experienced teacher.

─────────── ◊ ───────────

IN BUDDHIST MEDITATION TWO
ELEMENTS ARE USUALLY IDENTIFIED:

- **Samatha** – *tranquillity*
- **Vipassana** – *insight*

─────────── ◊ ───────────

In samatha, the practitioner brings all of the attention to bear on a single object, to the exclusion of all else. In vipassana, by contrast, the mind is opened and the practitioner watches, in a spirit of neutrality, all the various thoughts, desires and emotions as they rise and pass away.

Through the practice of meditation, the practitioner arrives at a state of being that is quiet and uninterrupted by transient preoccupations and concerns.

Although formal meditation is typically practised in an undisturbed situation for a prescribed period of time, there is a sense in which meditation can be brought to bear on other activities. For example, the Vietnamese Zen teacher Thich Nhat Hanh, among others, advocates driving meditation, telephone meditation and eating meditation. Walking, as well as sitting meditation, has been a characteristic of a number of Buddhist schools for many centuries.

The Spread of Buddhism

During the centuries immediately after the Buddha's death, the Sangha divided into eighteen different regional schools, each sharing a veneration of the Buddha and his teachings but evolving in different ways. Then, in the third century BCE, the movement spread dramatically due to the conversion of the Emperor Ashoka, in north India. Ashoka had just punished a rebellious group of subjects with a reign of terror, and was deeply affected by the bloodshed he had created. When he chanced upon a Buddhist monk,

⊙ ABOVE *Many young children are given over by their parents to a Buddhist way of life. This young boy is already taking advantage of a contemplative world.*

Nigrodha, he realized that he could use his immense power to promote peace. He converted to Buddhism, performed many charitable works, and had edicts carved in rock across his empire, exhorting his people to act generously and abhor violence. In place of armies, he sent missionaries far and wide to spread the Dharma, enjoying lasting success in Sri Lanka, where the Theravada tradition still flourishes.

The patronage of Ashoka did much to establish Buddhism as a popular religion. Later, the support of the Greek king Menandros (c.155–130 BCE) in the north and the Scythian leader Kanishka (first century BCE) in the north-west continued the tradition. In the south, scholars of the Theravada school in Sri Lanka committed their entire canon to writing during the first century. This became known as the Pali canon. Of the original eighteen schools, only this school has survived; from Sri Lanka, it was then to spread across south-east Asia.

During the fifth century CE, the Gupta Dynasty recognized Buddhism, and centres began to grow in number, with an increasingly intellectual orientation. By the seventh century there were four major Buddhist universities across India. But this was to be the religion's high point, for by the beginning of the thirteenth century, Muslim invaders had driven out most monks and scholars. Many went to the kingdoms of the Himalayas: Nepal, Sikkim, Bhutan and Tibet. More than six hundred years passed before Buddhism made a comeback in the land of its birth.

Mahayana and Hinayana/Theravada

During the first century CE, there was a flowering of thought in south and north-west India, influenced by both the Mediterranean and Arab worlds. This led to the development of 'Mahayana' Buddhism. 'Mahayana' means 'Great Vehicle' and was used in contrast to what had gone before, which was classified as 'Hinayana', or 'Lesser Vehicle', and was associated with the Theravada school. Hinayana, or Theravada, Buddhists taught that nirvana can only be achieved through strict control, self-denial and self-discipline; the proponents of Mahayana advocated rather that the potential for awakening dwells within each of us and only needs to be developed. Leaders of the Mahayana school introduced the notion of compassion, or karuna, as being as important a virtue as wisdom, or prajna. The notion of Emptiness, or Shunyata, meaning that everything is empty of independent existence, also became a fundamental aspect of the teaching. So too did the distinction between two kinds of truth: conventional, or everyday truth, and absolute, or ultimate truth.

⊙ MAIN PICTURE *The Temple of the Tooth in Kandy, Sri Lanka, is the spiritual heart of Theravada Buddhism. Sri Lanka is the centre of Theravada Buddhism, and it was from here that it spread to south-east Asia.*

In subsequent centuries, Hinayana Buddhism spread southward from Sri Lanka to Burma, Thailand, Laos, Cambodia and Indonesia. In recent years, Communist revolutions have wrought deep damage to the Buddhist communities in Burma, Laos and Cambodia; in Indonesia, however, both the Theravada and Mahayana schools now flourish.

While Theravada took root in southeast Asia, it was the Mahayana teachings that prevailed in countries to the north of India, among them Bhutan, Sikkim, Nepal and Ladakh. Mahayana teachings also spread to China, Mongolia, Russia and Tibet, but have now been all but destroyed in these countries by the Communist movement. From China, the movement also extended to Korea and later to Japan.

Tantra

A further development took place within Indian Buddhism between the third and seventh centuries CE. Philosophically, Tantra shared the Mahayana position on Shunyata; what made it distinctive as a school was its original method. In its use of ritual and its meditative practices, tantric teaching was greatly influenced by the ancient Vedic traditions of the Aryans who had occupied north India centuries earlier, and there was much cross-fertilization between north Indian tantric Buddhist practice and the teachings and rituals that are part of Hinduism today.

Tantra focuses on transforming the gross body by means of complex practices, which requires a special relationship with a guru, or spiritual teacher. Sexual symbolism is a prominent theme in both Buddhist and Hindu

⊙ MAIN PICTURE AND ABOVE *Brightly coloured prayer flags can be found wherever Tibetan Buddhists are. A young monk reads a prayer book (inset) at the Langmusi monastery, Gansu province, China.*

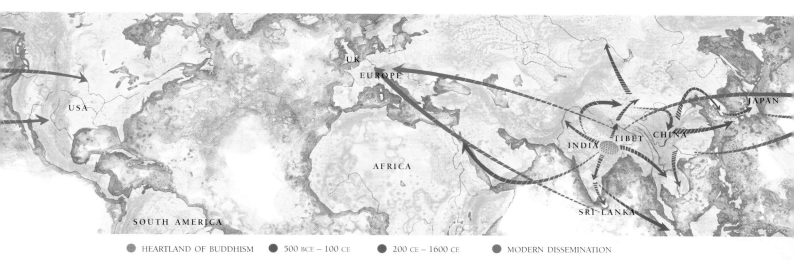

Tantra: both schools regard the male/female union as a conscious expression of the way back to unity from the initial male/female divide that set the creative process in motion and led to fragmentation of consciousness.

Tantra flourished in north India until the armies of Mohammed sent Buddhism into a decline. It also spread to Tibet, Mongolia and Siberia. Since the Chinese invasion of Tibet in 1959, many tantric teachings from the Tibetan tradition have become widespread for the first time across Australasia, Europe and North America, in

⊙ RIGHT *With the introduction of Tantra came the introduction of new deities; this ferocious 17th-century statue is believed to depict Hayagriva.*

particular the Dzogchen ('great perfection') teachings of the Nyingma school. Tantra also extended through China to Japan, where it survives today as the Shingon school.

Dhyana (Ch'an or Zen)

As Buddhism travelled to new countries with their own distinctive climates and cultures, it was inevitable that it would alter in accordance with the nature of the

⊙ ABOVE *A world map showing how Buddhism has gradually spread across the globe.*

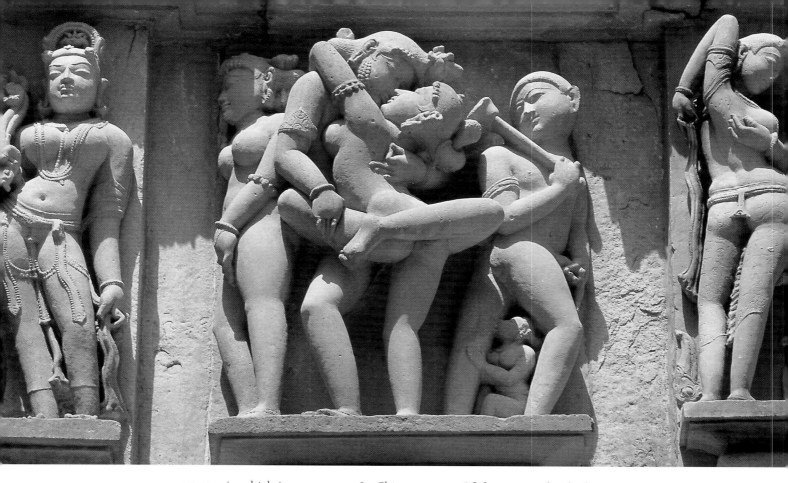

country in which it was a guest. In China, it was adopted both by ordinary people and by the authorities, and became the official religion until the tenth century, when the Tang Dynasty came to power and promoted Taoism and Confucianism. Nevertheless, it was to remain an active religion in China until the cultural revolution of 1966.

Of the many schools that sprang up during the transmission of Buddhism in China, Ch'an is a unique tradition that owes much to the down-to-earth character of the Chinese people, who were more pragmatic and less given to metaphysical tendencies than their Indian neighbours. The emphasis of Ch'an is to set aside book

⊙ ABOVE *These erotic Tantric Buddhist figures, over a thousand years old, form part of the striking facade on the Lakshmana Temple in Khajuraho, India.*

learning and dialectic and concentrate instead on 'buddhahood', or 'direct pointing to the heart of man'. The tradition was transmitted from master to disciple, from heart to heart. However, it should be emphasized that the rejection of scripture was not absolute; many original Ch'an texts appeared over time.

Ch'an teaching is characterized by sometimes radical tactics on the part of the teacher, who may use a variety of methods to awaken the disciple. Early Chinese masters lay great emphasis on the 'non-abiding mind' – the mind that rests nowhere, beyond all thought and relativity. From the words of the founder of Ch'an and subsequently Zen Buddhism, Bodhidharma, we have a succinct description of what Ch'an is:

A special channel outside the scriptures
A reliance outside of words and letters pointing directly to Mind
Seeing one's self in, and as, nature and attaining Enlightenment

Zen in Japan

Buddhist teachings first came to Japan from Korea during the sixth century CE. Not long after this, increasing numbers of Japanese Buddhist scholars also started to turn to China, and the leading six Chinese schools were all transplanted to Japan during the next five centuries. However, in Japan these schools tended to be the preserve of the elite, and so came under threat in the twelfth century, when the samurai, or warrior class, overthrew the decadent imperial aristocracy. In this new climate, more accessible and straightforward practices started to gain ground, among them Zen Buddhism.

The Zen school places supreme emphasis on self-power, and on the ability of the individual to galvanize his or her energies towards self-realization. The sometimes ruthlessly pragmatic approach of Zen masters won favour with the new samurai elite, for it provided them with a way of facing death with equanimity, and the emphasis in its method of responding spontaneously to the spirit of the moment could be transferred very effectively to military tactics and practices such as archery, sword play and wrestling. Conversely, the military tactics of the samurai themselves fed into the development of Zen. At the same time, the principles of spontaneity, simplicity and understatement flowered in the arts, bringing a distinctive style to calligraphy, ink painting, flower arranging, poetry and pottery, as well as to interior design and to the tea ceremony.

Two Zen schools – Rinzai and Soto – were brought by Chinese Ch'an masters from China to Japan. Of the two, Rinzai is more goal-oriented and militant in character. In addition to 'zazen', or sitting practice, it employs 'koan' – seemingly illogical questions – as a way of pushing the student beyond ordinary thought patterns. The Soto school also stresses the importance of zazen, but is more straightforward. For the Soto practitioner, enlightenment is just as likely in the rice field as in the meditation hall. In the words of its founder, Dogen:

To study the way is to study the self
To study the self is to forget the self
To forget the self is to be enlightened by all things

Buddhism in Tibet

The first Buddhist teachings reached Tibet during the seventh century CE. Tibetan spiritual practice prior to this time was animistic in orientation, with shaman-like priests, or bön-po, and a strong emphasis on magic. Legend has it that the demonic

⊙ LEFT *The Buddha in a typical mudra standing pose. This statue dates back to the Middle Edo period in Japan.*

spirits of the Tibetan plateau did all they could to resist the infiltration of Buddhism, and the eighth-century Tibetan saint Padmasambhava is credited with having had the necessary occult skills to placate these forces, and ensure that Buddhist teachings could take root. Padmasambhava did not expel the demons – instead he converted them, an approach which typifies one of the differences between the Buddhist and Christian traditions.

During subsequent periods, the principal schools established in Tibet were the Kadam ('bound by command') school; the Sakya school, named after its principal monastery in southern Tibet; the Kagyu ('transmitted command') school; the Nyingma ('old ones') school; and the Gelug ('virtuous') school. All combined Mahayana Buddhism with local Tibetan beliefs in idiosyncratic ways. Meanwhile, the indigenous Bon tradition took shape as a more organized religion in its own right, absorbing various Buddhist precepts in doing so.

A special aspect of Tibetan Buddhism is the role of the lama, or spiritual teacher. The lama's guidance is considered essential if the disciple (chela) is to navigate the perils of the spiritual path. In some cases, the lama is held in even higher regard than the Buddha, being seen as the embodiment of Ultimate Enlightenment. Also distinctive is the use of the mantra *om-mani-padme-hum* ('hail to the jewel of the lotus'), repeated by Buddhists of all schools and, prior to the Chinese invasion of 1959, inscribed on rocks, flags and prayer wheels across Tibet.

⊙ MAIN PICTURE *The Tibetan saint Padmasambhava, whom it is believed possessed the necessary occult powers to ensure that Buddhism took root in Tibet, not by expelling the demons fighting against it, but by converting them.*

Buddhism in the Modern World

During the course of the twentieth century, Buddhism has declined drastically in Asia, partly due to the materialistic emphasis of modern consumer culture, and partly because of the devastating impact of successive Communist revolutions whose leaders have done their best to eradicate all kinds of religious practice. However, at the same time, Buddhist teachings have started to flourish in the West. Today, there are Buddhist centres across Europe, North America and Australasia, with the number of converts growing every year. One interesting feature of Buddhism is that it does not seek to proselytize: many seekers of different traditions are actively encouraged by teachers such as the Dalai Lama to apply the benefits they find in Buddhist practice to their own religious tradition, if they wish to do so. Another emergence is an increasing dialogue between Christian and Buddhist leaders, giving many westerners food for thought about the basis of their understanding of what it really means to be a Christian.

⊙ ABOVE *The wonders of modern technology: a French nun listens to a translation of the words of the Dalai Lama at the Kalachakra ceremony in the Tabo monastery, Spiti.*

In the modern, individualistic consumer cultures of the West, Buddhist teachers from traditional Asian cultures have had to review the validity of their methods in the context of lifestyles and different ways as new teachers come forward and more lay people choose to express their commitment to the teachings through social and community programmes. Embraced today by people in

values that are often markedly different to those of the societies into which they were born. In all probability, the next century will see Buddhism continue to evolve in many walks of life, Buddhism remains a tradition which is open to all. I hope that the reflection cards will help you to use the teachings in a way that enriches your life.

⊙ MAIN PICTURE AND ABOVE *This beautiful, serene Buddha on the Lotus Road in Colombo, Sri Lanka, offers peace and calm in today's hectic world.*

How to Use Everyday Buddha

*I*n the same way that you have been drawn to these reflections, so I was drawn to the reflections of my own teacher. It was He who inspired me to look further and bring the teachings of the Buddha to a wider audience through the same medium.

Included in this pack are 366 cards, offering a reflection for each day of the year. I have drawn the reflections from a number of sources, chiefly 'The Dhammapada', widely regarded as the most accurate of the recorded versions of the Buddha's teachings. Extracts from 'The Dhammapada' account for the reflections on 288 cards, where the chapter and verse are shown. The remaining cards offer reflections from a variety of established texts – each of which are referenced – attributed to the Buddha. I studied numerous versions of all the texts referenced, including 'raw text' translations, and came up with my own interpretations. I hope they meet with your approval.

In this pack you will also find a mandala poster. Mandalas are used in certain Buddhist schools as part of initiation ceremonies or as symbolic maps of the spiritual universe. As you focus on the reflection on your card, see if you can trace a path through a section of the mandala, and if it can help you move deeper within the meaning of the words – and your own path.

Once you have assembled your altar – simply fold over the front cover along the crease and tuck the flap behind the back of the tray in which the cards sit – thoroughly shuffle all the cards, to make sure that your card selection is random.

Before you choose a card, sit quietly for a few minutes and collect yourself. Try to find a time and a place free from interruptions. Now draw a card from the pack. When you have read it, consider whether it relates to you and where you are with your life at this moment. Maybe the message is one you like; maybe it makes you feel uncomfortable. Whatever your first response, give yourself time to absorb it, and take it with you into the activities of the day. You may find that its significance reveals itself at an unexpected moment, or comes back to you when it is the furthest thing from your thoughts.

Perhaps you will only wish to draw a card once a week or month, or when something special is happening in your life. Perhaps you would like to meditate on the message for a short while, or for a longer period of time. Maybe you would like to carry the card in your purse or wallet and look at it for as long as you feel its message is valid. Maybe it will be valid for the rest of your life. As the Buddha taught, there are no rules. Everything is completely up to you.

Further Reading

The *Dhammapada* exists in many versions, each slightly different. Choose one that appeals to you from your local bookstore. To find out more about Buddhism, the following list provides a good starting point.

Batchelor, Stephen, *The Awakening of the West*. Albany, CA: Parallax Press 1994

Boorstein, Silvia, *It's Easier Than You Think*. Harper San Francisco, 1997

Boucher, Sandy, *Opening the Lotus*. NY: Ballantine Books, 1998

Chodron, Pema, *When Things Fall Apart*. Boston, MA: Shambhala, 1997

The Dalai Lama, *Freedom in Exile*. Harper San Francisco, 1998

Hagen, Steve, *Buddhism Plain and Simple*. Boston, MA: Charles E. Tuttle, 1997

Harvey, Peter, *An Introduction to Buddhism*. Cambridge University Press, 1990

Kiew Kit, Wong, *The Complete Book of Zen*. NY: Penguin, 1998

Kornfield, Jack, *A Path with Heart*. NY: Bantam Doubleday Dell Publications, 1993

Low, Albert, *An Invitation to Practice Zen*. Boston, MA: Charles E. Tuttle, 1989

O'Haloran, Maura, *Pure Heart, Enlightened Mind*. Boston, MA: Charles E. Tuttle, 1994

Okumura, Shohaku and Dan Leighton, *The Wholehearted Way: A Translation of Eihei Dogen's Bendowa*. Boston, MA: Charles E. Tuttle, 1997

Senzaki, Nyogen and Paul Reps, *Zen Flesh, Zen Bones*. Boston, MA: Charles E. Tuttle, 1998

Trungpa, Chögyam, *The Heart of the Buddha*. Boston, MA: Shambhala, 1991

Useful periodicals include *Tricycle* and *Shambala Sun*.

Useful Addresses

For a complete guide to centres in your area, refer to *The Buddhist Directory* compiled by Peter Lorie and Julie Foakes (Charles E. Tuttle, 1997).

BUDDHIST ASSOCIATION OF U.S.A.
3070 Albany Crescent
Bronx, NY 10472
Tel: (718) 884 9111

FRIENDS OF THE WESTERN BUDDHIST ORDER
Arya Loka Retreat Center
Hartwood Circle
Newmarket, NH 03857
Tel: (603) 659 5456

RIGPA FELLOWSHIP
449 Powell Street
Suite 200
San Francisco, CA 94102
Tel: (415) 392 2055

Acknowledgements

AUTHOR'S ACKNOWLEDGEMENTS
I would like to thank Tessa Strickland for her help with this project, which has gone far beyond that of a conventional agent/client relationship, and also Dr Stuart Rose for his invaluable assistance. I must mention the excellent people at Eddison Sadd who have worked very hard with what seems like never-ending enthusiasm on producing the finished article. Of course, the inspiration and guidance has come from my beloved teacher Sri Sathya Sai Baba, without whom my life would still be an empty shell.

PICTURE CREDITS
Bridgeman Art Library 12; E.T. Archive: Lucien Biton Collection Paris 27 / Musee Guimet Paris 8 *(inset)*, 9 *(inset)*, 15; Eye Ubiquitous: Tim Page 28–29, 29 *(inset)*; Images: Colour Library 18–19 / The Charles Walker Collection 9, 23, 24; Schoettle Collection, Joachim Baader, Munich: mandala poster and card detail; Tony Stone Images: Keith Bernstein 20–21 / Rich Iwasaki 13 / Joel Simon 2–3 / Hugh Sitton 20 *(inset)*; Tibet Images: Brian Beresford 7, 17 / B. Luther 4–5, 11 /Ian Cumming 6, 8, 10, 22 (& *inset*), 28 *(inset)*, 32 / Jirina Simajchlova 17 *(inset)*; Werner Forman Archive: Philip Goldman Collection, London 16 / Shirley Day, London

26, Victoria & Albert Picture Library: front cover.

EDDISON•SADD EDITIONS
Editorial Director......Ian Jackson
Senior Editor.........Tessa Monina
Proofreader.........Michele Turney
Art Director.....Elaine Partington
Senior Art Editor....Pritty Ramjee
Map Illustration......Andy Farmer
Production....Karyn Claridge and Charles James

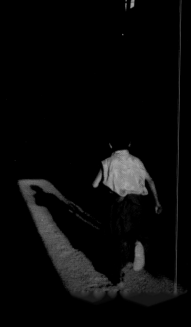